Driving In The

Rain

By

Nadia Bruce-Rawlings

Punk ★ Hostage ★ Press

Driving In The Rain

Edited by Iris Berry

Assistant Editor – Michele McDannold

Introduction by Rob Simbeck

Cover Photo by Denise Cordner

Cover Design by Michele McDannold

Punk Hostage Press
Hollywood, California
punkhostagepress.com

For Brian and Carlos

Author's Acknowledgements

Thank you so much to my sister Denise Cordner
for her gorgeous cover photo as well as the
Author's photo! And for being there for me
through thick and thin. I love you.

To my husband Brian Rawlings who has cared for
me through 13 surgeries and two autoimmune
diseases. Your love has kept me going.
I love you so much.

To all six of our kids for putting up with my
goofiness and writer's moodiness!
I love each of you.

To Darby Walker and Marilyn Moore for loving
me through it all and being the best friends a
woman could ask for. I love and miss you.

To Michele McDannold for the cover layout and
for making this book look so amazing. I miss you!

And last but certainly not least,
to Iris Berry and Punk Hostage Press,
for her patience and love, for our midnight editing
sessions, for holding my hand when I was filled
with doubt, for her perfect eye. And did I mention
her amazing patience? You are my mentor
and a true friend; I couldn't ask for more.
Thank you, I adore you.

Introduction

Addiction, recovery, and the forces that drive them make for some of literature's most compelling reading. Those of us who seek others' reflections on the often-horrific path toward death or redemption have a treasure trove to visit and revisit, from Baudelaire to Bukowski, Dorothy Parker to Anne Sexton. Every such work is a travelogue, and the journey, on the continuum from AAA magazine to The Divine Comedy, is only as interesting as the writer who has lived and is telling it.

Add Nadia Bruce-Rawlings's compelling *Driving In The Rain* to the list of must-reads. Like her harrowingly powerful first book, *Scars*, it is an episodic trip through scenes from a life that moves from family dysfunction through low-bottom addiction to recovery in all its challenging complexity.

The daughter of a troubled, hard-drinking oil executive and a mother who provided a counterbalance of joy and color through the veil of her own depression, Bruce-Rawlings brings a clear-eyed rigor to each piece, from the most impressionistic poem to the most detailed rumination on people and events. With great control of tone and a gift for the telling image, she takes us from childhood scenes in Egypt, with servants and vacations on Cyprus, to the most sordid of L.A. streets, from parties in Cannes and karaoke in Tokyo to stealing batteries and pregnancy tests to support her crack habit and sharing day-care motherhood with strippers. She is fearless in presenting both worlds and sketching the twilight zone between them, showing us that the struggles of adolescence in a dysfunctional family in the Middle East have their counterpart in the daily struggles of an addict, equally a foreigner in the surface world of respectability in any American city.

The writer's task is to turn words into recognition, then identification and emotion, and Bruce-Rawlings does it superbly. And when the events are as jarring and disorienting as they sometimes are here, she also needs to reassure us as we walk through each circle of hell. It is only honesty and strength that can do that as she uncovers truths about herself and about us, reminding us that at whatever stage of life, of dysfunction or recovery, we are on this thin raft together.

It is obvious she is still working through some of the scenes at hand, but she speaks as a survivor, and just as it is the journey that is the story, it is the destination—recovery—that makes it bearable and meaningful, and she has indeed come out the other side, bringing us with her as we read her. To hear stories of hazy moments in the arms of Lethe from someone who is clear-eyed and functioning is to see the human spirit triumphant. Turning horror to hope, as we have seen in so many tales that have held our attention through the ages, can give even the most sordid journey a golden destination, and it does so here.

~ **Rob Simbeck**, author of *Daughter of the Air: Brief Soaring Life of Cornelia Fort*

*I like to tell stories. I am going to tell you a story
about a girl who didn't want to belong.*

~ **Sandra Cisneros**
  The House On Mango Street

Driving In the Rain

I remember when I was still
new to sobriety
And the baby was maybe a year
I'd go driving in the rain
when she couldn't sleep
I'd go east on Pico instead of west
Toward the old stomping grounds
Toward MacArthur Park and crack town
I didn't go to score
Just to flirt a little with danger
Just to stroke that ex addict ego
Just to touch danger's cheek
Driving in the rain
Telling her it was an adventure
But really trying to get her to sleep
An adventure for danger
To feel my heart pound again
I'd see my old dealer
And go on past
Driving in the rain
Flirting with danger
Remembering the pain
But embracing the love

Baby, Things Change

Listening to Dwight, and
Yes, baby, things change.
Wondering if he's faithful
Wondering if I could ever be untrue
But some things should never be said out loud

Crying as I'm driving,
Knowing I'm too ashamed of my fat
To ever do that
But wanting a kiss or just a first touch
Some things, though, should never be
said out loud

No tender glances, no wildness
in the afternoon
No more electricity, just bills and chores
and, sometimes,
Quietly looking at the moon
Some things should just never be
said out loud

From Cannes

to Crack

"Do you work?" Susan asked.

I said, "No, not right now...I used to work as Director of International Sales in the film industry..." Susan was a hooker with an abscess the size of Texas on her leg. We were smoking in our dealer's room, room 112 at the Sunset Inn in Echo Park. A grand and beautiful venue.

Susan and Tom exchanged amused glances…"That wasn't what she meant," said Tom. Tom was a booster, about 60 maybe, with missing teeth and was just skin and bones. He stole better than anyone I'd ever seen, with a nonchalance I envied. He hadn't checked in with his parole officer in months. I was confused…

Tom said, "Are you working the streets?"

And finally it dawned on me. I was so out of my damn element here at the Sunset Inn. Lost and confused and desperately wanting a hit of crack. No, I wasn't a hooker, just an ex-film executive lost in a crazy world of boosting and crack. I used to go to Cannes, I wanted to say, but I knew they wouldn't have a clue what I was talking about. I used to go to Cannes and set up our office suite in the Carlton Hotel on La Croisette. Rent a Mercedes and cruise up to Monte Carlo with the bosses. Wear party dresses and hobnob with the stars. How the hell did I end up here on Sunset Blvd., smoking out of a broken pipe and waiting for my dealer to throw me a dove, a twenty or two? This wasn't my life. Wasn't my destiny. But somehow, someway…here I was.

I'd grown up an oil brat, moved all over the world, lived a life of leisure and luxury with a drunken dad who liked to abuse our mother. But still, it wasn't all that bad. Egypt for elementary and junior high, Norway for high school, college in Colorado after a failed suicide attempt in Philly. I usually had money, and if I didn't, daddy was just a phone call away.

The 80s were when I moved to LA, and the 80s brought cocaine and champagne my way. Along with millions of other folks. Till it became too much, and I was missing too much work. I told my dealer not to sell to me anymore and went off the coke. For five years all I did was drink and a few pills here and there. But a lot of drinking. Waking up hugging the toilet kind of drinking. Till I met a model in Italy on a work trip. He modeled for Armani, handsome as could be. Did a lot of cocaine. I didn't want to go back to that, but then again…

I didn't know where to buy coke anymore, so we went down to Hollywood and asked around and immediately found rock. I'd done it in Denver, ages ago, briefly, when we called it freebasing and thought we were high-falutin'. So...me and the model, we smoked us some crack. And boy, did I love it. I loved it so much; I wanted more in a minute.

My mom got sick with cancer, and I was going back and forth to Playas de Tijuana where she was in a holistic treatment center.

I would bring rocks of crack and a pipe over the border into Mexico every night so I could smoke. I would steal my boyfriend's debit card and go hang out with the homeless and smoke all night. I was working briefly at a small distribution company and would smoke in their bathroom. After our car got repossessed, I would borrow my boss's Mercedes to go score in MacArthur Park on my lunch hour. And then my mom died, one sad and lonely morning in Playas de Tijuana.

I held her hand and wished for crack. I settled for a beer for breakfast instead. By the time I got back to Los Angeles, I'd sunk into a deep depression. All I could see when I slept was my mother's face, grimacing as death took her, small flecks of blood on her teeth. I'd jerk awake, crying and terrified. I grew to hate sleep, and so I smoked more and more crack every night, avoiding sleep and the nightmares it brought.

And suddenly I wasn't going to Cannes or Milan anymore for work. Suddenly I weighed 95lbs and couldn't keep a job. I was on disability for depression, and I would sleep all day and smoke all night. While scoring, I stumbled across Walter, a tall Black homeless man who took care of Tom, the grand-master booster, and suddenly I was his driver. And suddenly there I was, boosting as well and hanging out in the Sunset Inn in Echo Park, proud that I wasn't a hooker too.

Mornings in Cannes were delicious, and occasionally California would remind me of them...when we went to Ventura County to boost and would travel near the beaches. I'd remember those days when life was good and I still looked pretty and healthy. One time I had the stomach flu and almost threw up on Peter Weller at the New Line party. Instead I hit the taxi door with vomit and knew enough French to tell him I wasn't drunk and to throw him a decent tip. Not a great example of the good old days, perhaps, but something I'll never forget. Eating like a queen, going to Madonna's party with the head of Showtime's acquisitions department. He brought me a rose every morning during the Festival. Going to Japan and seeing McCoy Tyner at the Blue Note, riding the Japanese trains with my boss and talking about life. Life then was good and healthy and wholesome. The film market in Milan was in the autumn, it was the gypsy circus and the high fashion. Seeing opera at La Scala.

I'd remember these moments as we drove from Rite-Aid to Rite-Aid, stealing batteries and makeup and pregnancy tests. I'd remember these moments when we got arrested, them asking me over and over where the guns were. I knew nothing about any guns, but they wouldn't believe me. And as I sat in Twin Towers jail for four months (several times), I day-dreamed that I was back in Cannes, sunning on the beach and eating a lovely salade Nicoise. Doing karaoke in Tokyo and eating sushi while we drank sake. My life had been pure and wonderful. Alcohol kept me going, of course, but that first hit of crack just dragged me down to hell.

Dealers

He called himself *El Chapin*, meaning a "Shorty" from Guatemala. He was at least 6'2", so the irony was obvious. It was before cell phones, but he gave me his number on a torn shred of notebook paper. He lived with Jose and his wife and kids, across the street from where I squatted. I was their best customer at times, when I was too lazy to go down to MacArthur Park to the wholesale dealer. I still don't know how or why the wholesaler did it—two twenty-dollar pieces for twenty bucks. And it was good stuff too. Ironically I ended up going to rehab across the street from his apartment house a few years later.

But *El Chapin*...he was tall and handsome and was sure I'd give him a blowjob for his crack. But I was a booster, not a hooker. He answered to Joaquin, the head of *La Mirada Locos*. Joaquin was a definite bad boy, handsome too but mean as hell. He had devil eyes. Rumors about him flooded the neighborhood. You did not want to be in debt to him, suffice it to say. Women who owed too much credit were raped and beaten, men were shot or beaten till they broke. There were certain nights the *Locos* took care of the debtors, and the neighborhood would be locked down tight.

69 was part of the cab contingency that delivered crack to the city. You called a cab company and asked for car #69; gave them your address; and voila, within 30 minutes one of three dealers would show up at your door with a bunch of crack. One driver (we called him "18" because he was 18th Street and had a

giant 18 tattooed on his chin), he had just had a baby with his girlfriend. So I would boost baby clothes and food for them to trade for crack. Great system. 18 seemed kind because he loved his baby so, but I'd seen what he would do to someone who'd crossed him. Of the three, Alberto was the best, and my most frequent dealer. Sometimes I'd ride with him and help keep him awake. He gave me the most credit, too, especially first thing in the morning before I'd had a chance to boost anything yet. He'd collect my debt in the evening when he started driving again. I never got too far into debt with him; he'd cut me off before I could. I'd given him my Green Card to hold for credit one night, and I got arrested the very next day. Spent hundreds getting a new one when I finally sobered up.

My dealer down by MacArthur Park, Pablo, would sometimes deliver. He drove a red Honda Civic, souped up and painted with white racing stripes, low-rider wheels and tinted windows. Subtle. I'd go to his apartment daily, he had the best stuff after the wholesale dealer. One time I went and knocked on his door, a 50-dollar bill folded neatly in my hand. The door was answered by a cop. They pulled me inside, handcuffed me and sat me on the couch. Pablo and his partner were handcuffed on the other couch, looking at me with fear and regret. I told the cops that I was there to pay Pablo for doing my brakes on my car, and that I didn't even know anything about the drugs. They didn't buy it for a minute, but thank God I had left my pipe in the car. I had nothing else on me, so they let me go. I stopped going to Pablo after that.

In Denver my dealers were white. Yvette worked with my boyfriend and me at a bar, and she was a speed freak who sold crack on the side. She had a great apartment, filled with people smoking crack and meth, using torches and giant pipes. Her dealer was Mark, and he eventually became our dealer too. I put the utilities for one of his safe houses in my name, and he gave me an eight-ball of cocaine for it. We spent sooooo much money with him. He carried a leather satchel filled with powder cocaine, carried it everywhere he went. He'd answer the door by pointing a gun at your head.

We spent all our free time with Mark and with Yvette, smoking, freebasing mounds of cocaine. I never ate. By this time I weighed 95lbs...I was 5'7". It wasn't cute. One morning I was reading the newspaper and came across an article about Mark and Yvette. It said he had been pulled over for a routine traffic violation. Apparently he grabbed a leather satchel from the car and ran. He made it to Yvettes apartment, where he held her and 2 others hostage for twenty-four hours. Finally, the SWAT team shot up the place, somehow managing not to kill anyone. It turned out he was wanted for first-degree murder. I realized all his utilities and his apartment lease were still in my name. We fled Denver within the hour, back to LA and our Hispanic dealers.

When I was locked up in LA, I made friends with Butterfly, a thin, pretty, half-white girl with a butterfly tattoo on her shoulder. Turned out her father was my Silverlake dealer whom I called Papi. He was old and commanded respect. His daughter, on the other hand, turned Aryan Nation while I knew her, beating up the black girls in our jail dorm.

I tried to stay away.

Upon release I went back to my squat in East Hollywood, across the street from Jose. *El Chapin* seemed to be gone. I got an insurance scam payout, and spent thousands that month with Jose. I knew I could get a better deal near MacArthur Park, but I was too loaded to get down there. His kids would open the door to me, the ten-year-old bringing me $100 worth of crack from the kitchen. When my insurance settlement ran out, far too quickly, I tried to get credit but only got laughed at.

So, I went back to Israel. Israel worked in Hollywood. He'd never done drugs and kept trying to talk me into going to rehab. He always gave me good deals, but dealt in too small quantities for my voracious appetite. I used him sparingly. One evening he was drunk, something he never was. He reached over to kiss me. He told me he was leaving the next day to go back to Texas, to get away from the life he lived. He begged me to go with him, go to rehab and start fresh with him. I thought about fucking him for some crack, but I hadn't showered that day and was embarrassed. I laughed as I did another hit. Israel begged me, told me he loved me and wanted a better life for both of us. But I knew I wouldn't, that I couldn't leave this life just yet.

Egypt...

So we had Egyptian food for lunch today. I lived in Egypt from 1974-1978, during the Peace Accord years, before Sadat was assassinated. I loved it. I was eight when we moved there; it was such a magical place for a little girl. I will never forget arriving at the airport, where a million people seemed to live. It was the middle of the night, and Mobil Oil had sent someone to meet our family and bribe our way through customs. We were whisked off into the night in a chauffeur driven car, surrounded by camels and donkey-carts and thousands of horns. I don't remember getting to the hotel (the Hilton or the Sheraton—we lived there for about 2 months waiting for our shipment to come from Texas). I do, however, remember waking up in the morning and looking out the window. It seemed we had been plopped into the middle of the most chaotic scene possible—streets overwhelmed by buses with no windows or doors, donkey-carts, camels, mopeds, cars, taxis...the lanes meant nothing. The cacophony of horns was astounding, really indescribable.

My memories of my childhood are very hazy, except the bad stuff, and I don't want this to be about pain. I don't really remember starting school there, but I do remember the school bus home to the hotel, and running in to the room because we always had the Pharaoh's Revenge. I remember slowly making friends. I remember our first house, a 100-plus year-old home in Ma'adi, with lush gardens and thick walls. We had a flat roof with turrets; I imagined myself a princess in a castle. Only, we were next door to a whore house, and my brother and father spent a great deal of time on the roof, looking with binoculars. We had grape vines and mango trees, and I would spend hours in the garden pretending to have a happy little family. I remember a friend whose house was equally fun to explore, and she had exciting dress-up clothes and old, mildewy books.

Later, when I outgrew the dress-up clothes and the fantasies, we would walk in Ma'adi and Digla, hiding in huge old sewage pipes and smoking cigarettes. We'd catch rides on the back of donkey-carts and yell at little Egyptian boys who would cuss at us and show us the bottom of their foot (a very rude gesture!). By 7th grade, I was drinking the Nefertiti wine that we would buy at the kiosk next to school, where the older kids bought hashish. I had a crush on Mark, who was a grade older than me and hung out with my older siblings. He kissed me once one drunken evening when we had snuck into the school compound. I remember what I was wearing, remember my shame at not wearing a bra, but honestly no one made them that small.

I remember going to Wimpy Burger and KFC—roach infested food that we thought was somewhat like home. The cokes and beers all had bugs in the bottles—you had to decant each drink unless you wanted a mouthful of insect. Today I find comfort in shawarma and gyros, hummus and tabbouleh, because it reminds me of my childhood, but back then I wanted European food.

At some point we moved from our grand home with the servant's stairs and maid's room and turrets, as my dad changed companies. We downgraded to a flat, though it was still awfully nice. I remember being really ill one day, having a giant fever and hallucinating, and having my mother try to comfort me with popsicles and cold rags. I always had strep throat then, for some reason. My brother had surgery on his foot, and they gave him some medication that made him hallucinate too. And my sister had mono for what seemed like months. It wasn't the healthiest of times.

I remember the Bread Riots, in January of 1977. According to Wikipedia:

The riots' origin lay in president Anwar Sadat's Infitah (openness) policy, which had, since he took power at the beginning of the decade, sought to liberalize the economy. In 1976, he sought loans from the World Bank in an effort to relieve the country's debt burden. The bank criticized the state's policy of subsidising basic foodstuffs, and Sadat announced in January 1977 that it was ending subsidies on flour, rice, and cooking oil and that it would cancel state employee bonuses and pay increases. The new policies resulted in a rise in the price of food by up to 50%.

For us, it was crazy—though I was too young to really understand. We had no school for several days, and a 24-hour curfew. My father had to stay at his office downtown, as foreigners were being shot at. The older kids snuck out, but I was too young, and my mom was too scared to let me out of her sight. It ended when the subsidies were put back, and we went back to life as usual.

I remember my first air raid warning— it was probably 1974 still, and a loud siren went off, and then all the electricity went out. My dad asked the house-boy if it was the *Yahudis* (the Jews — this was right after the '73 war with Israel). I knew instantly what that meant — air-raid warning! I'd read the *Diary of Anne Frank*, and my mom had told me about air-raids during her time in France in WWII. I was terrified. The funny thing was that no one bothered to tell me how long an air-raid warning lasted. I went to school the next day fully expecting to be bombed by the Israelis. Turned out we were safe.

We went to Sidi Abdel Rahman, near El Alamein, near Alexandria. It was a beautiful beach resort. I was with my mom and sister and brother, and their friends as well. We ended up having a sand storm, a *haboob*, for 5 days. It was crazy — you couldn't even see the ocean from our cabin which was just feet away. We spent a week there, getting cabin fever. My older brother and sister have different memories of this trip — they were camping with their buddies, I was in with our mom.

Every summer we'd go to Cyprus, without my dad. We'd spend some time in

Limassol and then several weeks in Pathos. It was amazing. What a way to grow up. When we weren't in Cyprus, we were in France visiting my mom's parents and sisters. And then we'd go to Canada for a few weeks as well, to shop and buy new school clothes. Again, it's all a bit hazy. I remember sandcastles and dunes and Aphrodite's Birthplace and Coral Bay, I remember blistered noses and volatile games of bridge. Great food. A Greek wedding. Beautiful sunsets and amazing people.

Today, I ate Egyptian food, and it brought back a flood of memories.

Fara, Fara, Fair as Light

I prefer to think of her like she was
the day I gave her my boots that fit her so
much better
Her laugh and lovely hair
Fara, Fara, fair as light

Her sparkling eyes and the little crooked tooth
We sat outside and watched the boats on the
lake
A little sweaty and her smoke hung in the
humidity
She told me of her life but it was no longer
filled with fight
Then, she was Fara, Fara, fair as light

I prefer not to think of her before she went
I prefer not to see it in my mind
Her sobriety chips lined up, all earned
with hard work and love
She'd told me of holding a gun in her mouth
but that was before, before she made it right.

Fara, Fara, fair as light.

I prefer not to visualize that day,
I prefer not to think her thoughts,
I prefer not to feel the metal weight
in her hand.
I prefer to remember the sunshine
in her hair and eyes,
not the shock and blood and pain and gone.
Fara, Fara, fair as light.

Happy Mother's Day

My mom would have been 82 today. She died in 1994 at the age of 58, in a cancer clinic in Playas de Tijuana, Mexico. The Gershon Clinic I think it's called. They did coffee enemas and a special alkaline diet. Sometimes it worked. We held out hope. But she died of pneumonia on August 4, 1994, at 4:30am. I had spent the night at the clinic that night, because the doctor told me he thought it was best. We had an air ambulance coming to take her back to Vancouver Island the next day.

I think she knew it was a waste of money and decided to leave before it came. I sat up all night with her, holding her hand and stroking her hair. She couldn't speak under the oxygen mask. But she held eye contact with me for hours it seemed, as if she had something really important to say. But I couldn't figure it out. Finally around 4am I took my book to another room and then fell asleep for a few minutes. It was then that she chose to die. I awoke to my father telling me she was gone. I was so confused, and then when it sunk in, I was so angry with myself for leaving her alone. I felt selfish. We went in her room, and as my dad took her puzzle ring off her finger to give to me, we closed her eyes. I noticed bits of blood around her mouth, around her teeth...as if she had gnashed her teeth when death came. It was horrible. For years after, I could not sleep. As soon as I closed my eyes, I would see that last image of my mother and my body would jerk awake, trying to keep her alive.

France was my mother's name—which was odd, because she came from France. She was born there in 1936, and grew up all over the world as her father was a diplomat with the French Embassy. She lived in France and New Zealand and Peru and London and other exotic places. She met her first husband and her second husband, both, in Tripoli, Libya. Her first husband was 15 year older than her. She had my brother and sister, and then he passed away from hypertension when they were only 3 and 2 years old. Can you imagine being a widow with two children at the age of 28 or so? She had moved to NY while he was ill, but then moved back to Tripoli to be with her family. There she met my father, who later broke her nose during a fight in Cairo, Egypt when I was 8 years old. He broke her collarbone too. We told everyone it had been a car accident. She wore a white cast on her nose and had two black eyes. Her arm was in a sling. That night my father had the audacity to tell me that no one had been hurt and that I shouldn't cry. I didn't really buy into that.

My mom was sweet and gentle and filled with laughter. But sometimes she suffered from depression, though she tried to hide that from us. My father drank alcoholically, and she tried to protect us from his fits of rage. I remember staying up all night listening to them fight, when I was just 7 or 8. They would come in my room and ask who I wanted to stay with. My dad would say he was leaving to go to a hotel, and he was taking me with him. My mom would say "No, she's staying with me." It went on for what seemed hours, and then in the morning we all pretended nothing had happened.

Later, my mom would hike and pick mushrooms and bird watch and raise snails in our garage. My friends in high school would come over and hang out with her, because she was so full of love and joy to them. She was there for my friend who got pregnant in high school and didn't know how to tell her very religious parents. She was there for me when I got my heart broken, and there for me when I did the heart breaking. She never judged, she just went on smiling and loving us. My father tore her down a lot, and it took years for her to build herself back up, but I like to think she had by the time she died.

When she got sick, we didn't think it

would be so quick, and we didn't really expect her to die. At least I didn't. I was starting my downward spiral into drugs. I'd met a guy who did cocaine, and gotten back onto that horror. Eventually, we started smoking crack. While my mom was dying in TJ, I would drive to San Diego and score and then come back, smuggling the crack across the border. A lot of it is a blur...drinking with my dad and then smoking with my boyfriend. And trying to hold it all together in front of my mom. It was madness. I was so scared of her leaving me. One day I came into her room, and she clearly didn't recognize me. The cancer had drifted to her brain, we believe. But it broke my heart. She tried so hard to be polite and cover it up.

When I was 15, she tried to kill herself. I didn't find out till my own suicide attempt at 18. She told me that when she had reunited with my father after being separated for a half year, she had realized he was still having one of his many affairs. She took every antihistamine in the house and then drank 2 bottles of wine. I remember that night because I had come home from my friend's house, in

Norway, and I had stayed up half the night talking to my mom who was crying and despondent. I had no idea at the time that she'd taken all the pills. I just thought she was drunk. She said I probably saved her life because I kept her awake that night.

I miss my mom. We had so much fun, when we weren't struggling against my father's crap. We would go to Cyprus every year with my older brother and sister. We'd play bridge and play in the water and travel the island. It was pure paradise. We'd go to France to visit my grandparents in Brittany. More beach, and castles, and just joy. In Cairo, we'd visit Sidi Abdel Rahman with her, where we got caught in a sandstorm for days, but frolicked on the beach when it was done. Later, when they retired to Nanaimo, Vancouver Island, we would walk the dogs on the beach for hours, and talk and talk. I called her almost every day. I see her now in my own daughter. Her laughter hasn't died.

A Memory Between

There's a memory between
The perfection of long hugs
Or a sweaty face mask
Social distancing
Or social climbing
Dancing slowly in the dark
Or one-way aisles in the market
There's a moment we lost
Waiting for the stimulus check
A moment we lost
When the restaurants closed
Moments gone
When pomp and circumstance was silenced
An argument in futility
With each political post
Absence of malice
Or malice in their absence
A meaningful life lost
Each time we fail to obey
Nothing will ever be the same

Howard

So when I was about 8 years sober, I finally was able to buy a home. I'd repaired my credit and made amends well enough with my father that he said he would help me with the down payment. So since I was living in Los Angeles, and it was sometime in 2006, the housing prices were insane. I didn't want to live in The Valley, so I started looking south of the 10 freeway, east of La Brea. I found an old home on 29th and Somerset, in the Crenshaw District. The Crenshaw District is in what used to be South Central - they stopped calling that area South Central and broke it up into little nice sounding districts at some point. Anyway, it was a 1920s Spanish art-deco home, with original tile and original everything. The sweet family who were selling it had lived in it forever. They had curtains that were actually thread-bare. And this amazingly old, faded, green carpet. It was clean, but it clearly needed some work. The real estate agent in charge of the Open House was this amazingly old, creased and bent-over African American gentleman. I was there alone—had just happened to drive by and see the sign. He was fascinated by me, I think, but happy to try to sell me the home. I fell in love! The next afternoon I brought my agent and my daughter, who both thought I was a little insane. I had the dream of what it could be in my head...they couldn't see it! But the agents did what agents do, and the mortgage man did miracles, and less than 6 weeks later I was signing the new house into my life.

Now...I had previously met this guy named Howard on Match. It turned out he had seen me before at an AA meeting. He, in theory, had like 20 years sober, was a contractor, and owned several homes but...he was living at home with his mom while he flipped one of the houses. That should have been my first clue. But like all sociopaths, he was very charming. He had two or three phones at all times, yet I could never reach him...he told me I called at inconvenient times. He got up at 4am to go work out, supposedly. Sophia told me he was mean to her, but I blamed that on jealousy.

Anyway, since he was a "contractor," I agreed to let him fix my new house for me. I was so excited. I had this vision, did I mention that? We needed to re-plumb and put in a central HVAC system, and a new roof, and some other stuff. I wanted to keep the charm of the place though. I wanted to remove the carpeting, and stain the wood floors underneath a dark stain. I picked out paint colors. It was going to be so gorgeous! We started arguing about money because he was being very cagey about telling me what he was spending and what he was doing. Our relationship was pretty much over, it was clear. We were communicating mainly through email because I could never reach him by phone. He texted me a picture of the tile he wanted to put in the kitchen...keep in mind this was 2006, we didn't have the greatest texting capability. So the picture looked ok, and I approved. Then...it was move-in day. I had told him weeks and days in advance of my move-in schedule. He promised all would be done, especially the wood floors.

So I arrive with the movers...and the wood floors are WET. I call him, but can't reach him. I'm freaking out. I call and call, and the movers are about to just leave all my belongings on the front lawn. So finally he calls and tells me to just put moving blankets down, or paper, and the floors will be fine. Hahahaaaa. Yeah. So we do this, and then I notice the HIDEOUS tile in the kitchen and art room. I mean, hideous. It was commercial, shiny, orange tile. I try calling him again, but no. So...what could I do? I keep moving and unpacking, on a wet floor that one of the movers told me had been painted, not stained.

Painted. And did I mention it was still wet? And that we're just messing it up? It had no top coat on it—he never did give it one. Later, even after it dried, when the sun shone on it in summer, it would melt and our feet would get stuck to it.

So, long story short—he scammed me out of about $70k. I was stupid and never got an actual contract from him, since we were in "love." But I decided to call the contractor's Board and make a formal complaint so that others wouldn't get harmed by him. And guess what? It turned out that he had lost his contractor's license more than two years prior. So, I filed a complaint. And as I told a few people about this, I found out that he had done this to many other women, and frighteningly, to a few men as well. The reason he didn't go to many AA meetings was that he was hated in the community because of the damage he had done to so many people.

When he found out I'd made a complaint against him with the contractor's board, he called DCS and told them that I beat Sophia, that I locked her in the closet for hours at a time, that I threw her against the wall, etc., etc. So, they came to visit me. They rang the bell that had a little homemade Peace & Love painting above it, and entered into a living room filled with art depicting various Mother & Child scenes. They went to check her closet, where I supposedly locked her, but found it had no door—instead it had hippie beads that had Peace and Love painted all over them. My closet had a door that didn't even close properly, certainly didn't lock. So...DCS decided the complaint was without merit. But...I still had to take her to the police station to get interviewed by a detective. The station in our jurisdiction was on Western and Martin Luther King Jr Blvd—a very, very scary area! I was this sad little white woman, with a little girl being taken down the hall by a uniformed police officer. It was crazy. Poor Sophia was only 5 or 6 and was terrified they were going to take her away.

Nowadays, my husband calls his Higher Power "Howard," because of the movie Stripes (when Bill Murray is saying the Lord's Prayer and says "...and Howard be thy name"). I keep telling him that's weird because Howard ruined my life (briefly), but he says that's not his business. Makes sense.

I ended up living in Crenshaw for several years, loving it so much. It was a great home. Howard and the DCS weren't able to ruin it for more than a moment. I finally got all his damage to the home fixed. We had to take the kitchen floor down past the sub-floor in order to repair what he'd done. Nice. But I found a real contractor who was great, and he made the home my favorite place to be. Sunshine could melt the floors, but only encourage the joy.

Linoleum Roses

Inspired By The House On Mango Street

Trapped in the tower that he bought
Better than Papa and the pain he wrought
Linoleum roses and a room full of pink
Hole in the door but no dishes in the sink
Hair in curlers till he comes home
Lipstick on fast and remember to moan
No visitors now because they might tell
Of how he's really just brought you to hell

Peace Accord

Originally published in the Spring 2018
edition of *Bluestem Magazine*.

My first bikini, polka dotted in blue, the
Cairo sun and the pee-scented pool. My mom's
bikini is brown polka dotted. She is so tanned
she looks almost Egyptian. The roly-poly
German ladies go topless even though it's the
Middle East, but we all know they have no
shame. My strawberry blonde hair is long and
wet with sweat and chlorine and hits my
sunburned nose. My nose is always peeling,

always bubbled up a little. We use Coppertone or baby oil to tan. I play in the mango garden under the grape vines when I want shade at our home, but at the Club we only want sun. I remember going to get grilled cheese sandwiches from the bar. Flat European bread and mango juice and a hot grill run by a teenaged Arab boy. I am so tall, but when he stares at my chest it makes no sense. The bikini ruffle, heavy with pool water, flutters open, and reveals my flat nipple. Laughter. I run. But I don't tell my mom…I made such a fuss to buy this bathing suit in Canada over the summer, along with the white nail polish she said was tacky and bourgeois. Too young for polish and probably too young for a bikini, and now the hot sun burns my shamed face.

Val and I play in the mud by the canal. She gets parasites, but she isn't as ashamed as my mother is when I get lice. Later Val and I drink alcohol by the tennis courts late at night, sneaking out of the outdoor movie theatre where we rent seat cushions for five *piasters* each. I carry her drunkenly home through the hot Cairo night. The soldiers and guards miraculously leave us alone, but her mother watches angrily while I pull her up four flights of stairs to her tower room next to a mosque. Call to prayer comes early, and she pukes in harmony to "Allahu Akbar." Her mother tells mine that we can never play together again.

Cigarettes from Abdul at the kiosk. Mark wears wife-beaters and bell bottoms and has a child back home, so they say. I am too shy to speak with him till alcohol numbs us both, and when he touches my flat chest I pray they'll suddenly grow. School time comes; I'm red with embarrassment. We never speak again. Stephen stands up for me when the other preteens call me pancake-chest, so I long for his gaze but Pam has a hold on him. Sherrie and I smoke in the huge abandoned sewer pipes, catching donkey rides from home in our shorts and halter tops. The veiled Arab ladies look away, the men stare, and the little Egyptian boys try to grab our asses. We've learned to insult them in their own language. Kos Omek...kos omek...kos omek. We chant, giggling. While Sadat and Begin sign the Peace Accord and shake hands, I hug our maid, who is my age and shares my name. We cry, holding each other, with happiness. Her husband, our cook, is as old as my grandfather. I ask how they could be married, and receive a red face similar to how red mine is when she has to clean the blood from our living room floor. My father has broken my mother's nose, but we tell everyone it was a car accident. Some things even friends can't discuss. Mom's collarbone is broken too, and we ignore the sling and the big white plaster on her face. *Ma'alesh*, says my dad, who takes binoculars to the roof to look through the windows of the whore house next door. We see soldiers going in there, holding hands with each other, and I am confused but laugh with my mom as if I understand. They wear machine guns slung over their shoulders, though we've been told the Egyptian government is too poor to issue ammunition. I find comfort that our maid Nadia and I share a name. I am sad, though, that she has to clean, and work, and wear robes, while I can run and play in shorts and halter tops. I remember getting small Nutella containers and fake cigarettes and wine from the kiosk near school, where the older kids bought hashish and real cigarettes. Ages seven through twelve are intertwined in a memory of sweets and wine and beatings and dust and camels and traffic and calls-to-prayer and overly chlorinated pool water and old spaghetti westerns.

When we first move there, right after the '73 war with Israel, Mom tells us to ignore everyone on the street, just keep walking. Walking back to our hotel; soldiers with machine guns yell at us, waving the guns in our direction, running toward us. Mom keeps us walking, "just ignore them!" My brother, panicking, finally gets her to see the weaponry as it is nearly shoved in our face. We stop just in time; apparently we are in a sensitive area in front of an off-limits building. In school, near the army base, we hear target practice all day. Half our classrooms then are prefabs. We get half-days as the weather heats up, and we take salt-tablets before gym class.

Walking through the Khan el-Khalili in downtown Cairo. There must be a million stalls, ten million customers. We're the only white people for miles. My parents move ahead of me, and I'm suddenly surrounded by women and children, stroking my long, strawberry blonde hair. I can't call loud enough for them to hear and finally they turn, startled by the crowd that has formed around their little girl but surprised by my tears.

We have mango trees, and guava, and bashmalla fruit, grape vines, all surround our garden, watered by Nile water from the canals. I'm warned to stay away or I'll get parasites like Val, but I don't understand and so I make mud pies by myself under the vines and lush trees. In less than a year, I will walk home alone from the Ma'adi Club after a movie. They run out from near the whore house, grabbing my pants, trying to get my zipper. I am just nine, but I understand these boys will hurt me. I scream at our gate, pound on the bell until the buzzer rings, and I scare off the boys eager to take my innocence.

Smells there are different; extreme. Light there is different; harsh white and glaring. Camel urine and cockroaches and dead rotting bodies and flesh of fruit that's been in the heat too long. Our rugs forever hold the smell. We walk past a car wreck where the bodies remain for days. The cops are busy shooting dogs and taking their left paw as proof of death, in the war against rabies. They leave the corpses for some other department, which never seems informed.

Sharm El-Sheikh is serene and lovely compared to Cairo, compared to Ma'adi. The ocean calm, the sand smooth and white, and we are ready for a week without our father. Neil Young and Led Zeppelin, my mother in her faded bell bottoms and tie dye, and we soak in the sun. Then the winds start, and the *haboob* begins, and days and nights make no difference. We are in a little cabin, unable to see anything but the sand blowing around us. The noise is impressive, and we dig into the wine and cheese and wait. It ends up lasting almost 6 days, so we eventually lose our minds playing bridge and checkers and yelling at each other. The last day there though…we are in heaven again, white sand, the wrestling teacher is there and has only half a leg. We make jokes and swim in the calm. Later that night our driver takes us home to Ma'adi, past Rommel's old abandoned tanks. They remind my mom to tell us stories of growing up in France during WWII, and we doze listening to her speak of the gestapo and of eating all the sugar ration early one month during the beginning of the war.

My father changes jobs when I am perhaps 10. He'd left Mobil Oil after twenty years there. We don't know exactly why, but there are hushed conversations late at night about his drinking. We spend a long, cool summer in Calgary, watching Nadia Comaneci win the Olympics. We are in someone else's home, a summer rental, and I dig through their daughter's carefully boxed belongings to gain a glimpse of what must be her perfect life. I remember riding her bike to ride to the 7-11 through the friendly suburban neighborhood, birds chirping, kids on lawns. It smells of pine and freshly cut grass. The 7-11 is resplendent in its wealth of shiny candy and sweets, no Nefertiti wine, but plenty of Sweet-Tarts to roughen my tongue. I pay for my candies with pennies that I stole from around the house, and suddenly I'm ashamed as I hand the clerk 100 pennies and a dime. I'm dressed in a denim overall dress, and I haven't put a shirt underneath, but the bib is just a tad too low. He notices this, as I blush. He's a nice Canadian young man, looking away quickly and reassuring me that they need the pennies.

The house in Calgary comes with a small white dog, a Westie that I sleep with. After a couple of months there, my step-grandmother comes to visit. My brother and sister taunt me because they have two fathers and more grandparents than me. That is, until the evening Grandma Bev gets drunk slowly in the kitchen, arguing with my mother. She needs help to bed, and suddenly her zebra-striped dressing gown comes open as she falls to the ground, exposing a naked body covered only by nude-shade pantyhose. I stare at her gray pubes and cry. My father shoos me away to my room where I listen to them struggle with her drunken ramblings. In the morning we all act as though nothing has happened, though she moans about her headache and avoids our eyes.

Finally, after much negotiating on my father's part, we end up back in Cairo just before school starts. He's taken a job with Canadian Superior Oil. I'm excited to go back, to start sixth grade, to see my friends. The plane door opens to that smell and that heat, and I know I am home again. This time though, no big house with a roof and turrets, no mango garden. We are in a flat with thin walls and no live-in maid. No more driver, but still a house boy and gardener. The heat shimmers in the distance, thick and slow. The house boy prays five times a day in front of the fridge and ignores my mother. No authority is recognized from a woman though, and my father is always gone. Eventually my brother has to fire him after school one day. The house boy would take it from a fourteen-year-old, but not from a woman. He toddles off on his broken bicycle, cursing my mother and all the infidel.

When the Bread Riots happen, we get off of school because of the danger and the curfew. They are shooting at people in Mercedes, because the Arabs drive much cheaper cars or ride on donkeys. My father stays at his office for a few days. My brother and sister sneak out during curfew, but I am too young as usual, and so I stay home with Mom. She cries and pulls out maps, asking me where we should move if she were to leave my dad. Over the summer in Calgary, they had fought over who would get custody of me and had asked me to decide. I cried, frozen. My mother asks me, "France, or maybe Greece, or maybe back to Canada, but definitely not Dallas, but we could live anywhere!" and I pretend to be excited because that's what she wants, but I just want to live somewhere safe and filled with love. I long again for the hugs from the other Nadia and for the sweetness of Sadat and Begin on our television, shaking hands.

PTSD

Crash of glass, and suddenly you're inside, and I yell to the kids to run downstairs, and you're grabbing my phone, and you throw it out the window, and you're screaming such filth, and there's spit flying out your mouth and you clutch my throat and how...how. You'd said you loved me. You smell like vodka and cigarettes, and your hands are cold around my neck, and it hurts, and you know about my metal plate, but you keep crushing anyway, and I can't breathe, and I'm out of my body and watching us struggle, and then finally your eyes touch mine for just a minute, and you...stop. I'm crashing against the counter, hitting my other surgery scar on the granite, and I run and scream and run and scream and scream and scream, and you are yelling more bile and laughing and telling me you'll destroy me, but how...how. You'd said you loved me?

Scattering Daddy

The Badlands are barren, dusty, and dank
The rocky levels, each era a different color
He loved their history, silent like him
Loved more than any person
And so we join his dust with theirs
We have fought and cried
And made up and tried
To be a family
Scattering Daddy

Every Day was Xmas

at Betty's

Betty hated the 4th of July. Every year she'd tell my daughter Sophia, and all the other little kids, about how her little sister had burned to death on that day. It had been early in the 20th century, long before they made kids' pajamas flame retardant. She'd been outside in the yard with a sparkler. Betty was about 7, her sister a bit younger. The sparkler sparked her nightie, and the rest made a very graphic story for little four-year-old daycare kids.

Christmas was another thing altogether. Every day was Christmas at Betty's house. She had a giant fake tree in the living room, year-round—decorated extensively and tackily. But she loved it, as did all the kids. It was a beautiful memento of her favorite holiday. She loved to go to the 99-cent store and buy hundreds of gifts for the little ones. Shoddy pink and blue toys from China that smelled like plastic and broke too quickly. But the kids loved to open the gifts. On birthdays they'd gather around the Christmas tree as well, opening all the gifts the birthday girl or boy had received from us well-meaning but broke parents.

Betty always meant well. She was the most loving woman with a heart the size of the world. In her eulogy, I said that she had wrapped generations of children in her arms, and indeed she had. Her love was palpable. Her home was filled with joyous laughter and screams of delight. But the walls were crumbling and some rooms in the back barely had floorboards. I was surprised she was able to get licensed year after year, but somehow she remained open.

Betty's son, Freddy, had married a wealthy doctor, but neither felt obligated to help out Betty. They were both joyous and loving as well, but Freddy clearly had some demons. I wondered about his childhood. Was his mother too busy with her daycare to look after her own kids? Her husband was a meat cutter. Her second husband, that is. Apparently her first husband was a bad man who locked her in the closet, amongst other not so nice things. But she adored her second husband. When he died, she was devastated for years on end. Unfortunately, her children didn't visit often, and so she found joy in her young clients and their crazy parents.

Betty would work from early morning till 6pm, loving the children with all her heart. At 6:30, when all the kids were gone, she'd sit on her front porch and have one cigarette and a small cola and whiskey. We'd often sit together, and she'd tell me stories of her life, growing up in Boston. My daughter grew to have a Boston accent. In fact, Sophia called me Betty long before she called me Mommy. It broke my heart.

All the families that went to Betty had a story, including me. There was the wild woman with pink hair, with two young kids from different fathers. She was constantly bouncing checks to poor Betty. There was Charles and Rebecca, who split up often in rather dramatic fashion. She was gorgeous but bipolar, and he worshipped her. They both went to AA meetings with me, and our daughters are best friends to this day. When their youngest, Lia, was three, she bit Sophia's arm and drew blood. Young love. There was the single mom who was a stripper and began having an affair with another stripper. Her daughter was five and would dance stripper moves in Betty's living room. There were two young helpers who'd both grown up going to Betty's daycare. They loved her like grandkids, and helped her with the little ones after school. Then when they went off to college, Rosa took over. She was amazing.

By then, Betty was starting to forget

things, though we all chose to ignore it. Rosa would find money Betty had hidden away and put it in Betty's bank account. She'd make sure Betty ate, something she often forgot. She'd pick up the "bigger" kids from school and walk them to Betty's and help them with homework, give them snacks, the whole nine yards. And then the parents would arrive, all with excuses why they couldn't pay that week. Betty would let them slide...she'd have me help her fill out the paperwork to borrow against her life insurance so she could keep afloat another month. One day her son Freddy found some paperwork she'd hidden in the linen closet. It seemed her mortgage payments were so past due that she was about to lose her home. She'd received the letter and hidden it, not wanting to face reality. By then she was forgetting more and more, and losing clients who were realizing what was going on. She had other health problems as well—a prolapsed bladder or uterus that she refused to do anything about. Because of it, she had constant urinary tract infections. It was horrible. For some reason her family did nothing about it, which angered me to no end. But I tried to get her to the doctor and soon learned she was impossible to argue with. Betty was the most stubborn woman I have ever met.

One morning Rosa came and everything was locked up tight. She had a key, so she let herself in, and found Betty still in bed, passed out almost. Rosa called her son, who got her to the hospital. Turns out she'd eaten nothing but Dove Bars for days and was very ill. At the hospital they did some cognitive tests, and found she had advanced dementia. We were all shocked, but really we'd all helped enable the lies. She'd often mix me up with Stacy, a strawberry blonde teacher who was as sweet as they come. Her daughter was one of the older kids who helped the little ones. She never knew what day it was, and sometimes talked about her husband as if he were still alive. But it was all little things, at least in our minds, and we didn't want to believe that Betty could be fading away. She was the grandma we all needed. But between the dementia and losing the house, it was inevitable.

And so one day, Freddy checked his

mom Betty into an assisted living damentia oriented home. I cried, the kids cried, the moms all cried. How could we live without our Betty, without the love that surrounded her home? How could we watch Betty die slowly but surely in this urine-scented center? The tragedy was that she was still cognitive enough to know what was going on, and she didn't like it one bit. A gentleman resident of her assisted living kept coming into her room in the middle of the night to take a dump. That one upset her the worst. Often I would go visit her at dinner time, and there were a couple of old women who would argue with each other at top voice, hitting each other with their canes and walkers. It was sheer insanity. The staff did nothing. It was comical to an extent, and then just became sad and tragic. My heart was breaking for sweet old Betty, who would complain she was stuck in this place with a bunch of old creepy people.

I was busy with work and life, and visited Betty less and less. Stacy, the other redheaded mother, visited often, and I would sometimes get credit for her visits because

Betty had long since stopped being able to tell us apart. I took the credit and felt guilty. Sophia was old enough now that she no longer needed daycare. The woman with whom she had spent more than half her life was fading and dying. Sophia had often stayed the night there, with her surrogate grandma, and when I went to London for a job interview, Betty looked after her for three wonderful days. We missed her so, but to visit was so depressing. At this point she could hardly leave her bed, and her laughter and smiles had long since faded.

Finally, one evening when I was visiting my now-husband Brian, I got the call. Betty's heart had finally stopped and let her join her husband in Heaven. Brian came into the room to find me sobbing hysterically. An entire era had just ended for me. Sophia was actually with Betty's grandkids, having a sleepover at Freddy and Michele's home. They were the ones who had called me. I said goodbye to date-night and drove down to Beverly Hills, trying not to sob so I could see while I drove. We had ice cream in Betty's honor and stayed up all night telling our favorite stories of the woman we had all loved so much.

Betty's funeral was filled with women and children who had loved her with all their hearts. I spoke at length about our love for her. It was my first Catholic funeral, and she would have loved it. It honored her well.

Tina

Tina would walk her dachshund for hours.

Tina. She was schizophrenic and refused her meds. Or if she did take them, they certainly didn't work. Tina was the spitting image of Ursula from The Little Mermaid. She was Asian, tall and overweight, with breasts that hung halfway to her knees. She always wore a dirty white bra with her boobs only half covered, and a tattered black nightie that was too tight. Her hair was in a bizarre knot on top of her head, with chunks of hair spilling

75

down her shoulders. Her makeup was the best…eyeliner like Amy Winehouse, but it missed her eyes and got all the way to her forehead. Her lipstick also missed, making a clownish bright red giant crooked mouth that emphasized her lack of teeth. And then, attached to a long leash, would be her little dachshund doggie, slowly walking with her regal charge.

Tina heard voices, and to cover them up she would play the rap radio station at full blast. She had a good stereo, and it made items inside my next-door apartment shake and rattle. One could hear nothing else. We lived in a four-plex, and we'd all try to get her to turn it down. Pounding on her door, we'd beg for some peace, but she'd just laugh at us. She'd pee in the lobby of the building whenever our other neighbor called the cops on her. Or just whenever she felt like it.

The most amazing thing about Tina was that she was married, with a young son about seven years old. Her husband was handsome. He drove a van for a charity that collected used toys for homeless kids. They would give my daughter presents on her birthday and at Christmas from the toys, always quite nice ones. Tina's husband was gone a lot, and really who could blame him, but he seemed to take good care of her and their little boy.

One time I was behind him in line at the pharmacy at Walgreens, and he was picking up her birth control pills. That meant they had sex…

Tina loved Sophia, and she'd often pop her head in my open window to say hello. It made Sophia, who was about three at the time, cry her little head off. Tina was a scary sight. Their landlord was a small Asian man who would periodically appear and clean up the apartment. We all had separate landlords, and none of us could figure out their relationship. Why did he let her live there? I finally got to talking with him once, when he was getting the apartment ready to sell. Tina and her family were moving out, God knows where, and he was doing some renovations. He was a family friend, had known Tina since she was a child. He said she was normal till her twenties, then she slowly began to change. That's when schizophrenia usually hits, apparently. I tried to press as to how she'd gotten married, but got very little from him. Apparently Tina's husband had gotten her pregnant and done the chivalrous thing and married her. And stuck around. He was a good man, but I just couldn't understand how he had ever been attracted to her and how he put up with her disease.

The sad thing was Tina's son. I never

learned his name. He was a good-looking little boy, polite and timid. I was sure he got bullied by the other kids. He never had friends over or played in the yard. I felt so badly for him. Tina would yell at him, and his father just seemed to ignore him. I know the neighbors had called Child Protective Services, but he was still there so I suppose the home wasn't so bad. I couldn't imagine anything worse though.

One night before she moved, instead of me calling the cops on her, she called the cops on me. I'd been pounding on her door, trying to get her to turn down the rap music that was moving my walls. So, she called the cops. I had finally given up and gone to bed, when there was a loud knock and "LAPD, open up!" came through my door. I put on a robe and went to open the door. The door that was still vibrating from her music. The cops looked confused that they'd been called to my place, not hers. I said, "Oh, she's crazy, she just doesn't like me today." So they checked my apartment to be sure all was good, then went to deal with her. The music was so loud that she couldn't hear them pounding on her door with their flashlights. They went around to her windows and knocked on them. Tina finally answered, and complained that I was making too much noise. They dealt with her while

I went to bed, comforted in the fact that she would soon be moving.

Girl Crush

Shawna wasn't my first girl-crush, but she was the first one I went ahead with. Well, while sober that is, and with no men involved. We were in rehab near MacArthur Park in Los Angeles, both started there around the same time. We came from similar backgrounds, unlike most of the other women there. I admired her photography, she admired my writing. I wanted to talk with her all night. We both had a hard time sleeping, being newly sober. At 3 or 4am we'd sneak out to the smoking area and talk and talk. I hadn't spoken to someone with a brain in years, it seemed. Someone who'd read the same books and listened to the same music. Done the same things. We were excited intellectually, and we were both horny as hell. When Shawna touched my leg, I felt a wave of electricity. The counselor saw her touch me, and we were banned from the smoking area until 6am from thereon in. So we'd meet in the laundry room, or the kitchen, or wherever we could manage a quick kiss and hug. We slipped notes to each other. It was like high school all over. Here we were in our mid-thirties, sneaking around trying not to get caught, hormones racing.

Shawna had a bit more time in the house than I did, so she could be my sober-escort to Doctor appointments and such. We'd go to the low-income clinic downtown and make out and hold hands while we waited. Everyone would stare because it was the 90s, and we were two women. I'd never done anything like that before...because, well, I was straight. It was so exciting and so forbidden that it made it even more exciting.

She was facing some serious time if Court didn't go her way, and I would worry for her every time she went to court. We had to write a Letter to God every day in the rehab, and mine were often focused on her, cleverly using her initials in case anyone read it. Thought I was so clever. Silly. But

I was so in love, I couldn't think clearly.

Something happened, and she and her other friend in the house thought I had ratted on her, or something like that. Honestly it's a bit hazy. But she stopped talking to me, and I cried for what seemed like weeks. I was devastated. And they wouldn't listen to my side of the story. They, of course, became lovers, and later when they graduated from the rehab they lived together. They married eventually, but finally heroin won, and her wife OD'd. It was a tragic story. I knew by then that Shawna and I were not meant to be together, but to this day I'm saddened by what happened at that rehab. The pain of losing my first girl crush at 32 was as bad as the pain of losing my first boy crush back when I was 13.

At some point, before her wife died, Shawna started to go through transitioning to become a man. I didn't know about it—we'd lost touch—but I would see them at my AA meeting every week and started to notice the changes. When we were together in rehab, she'd never discussed gender identity with me, and I had no idea she felt uncomfortable as a woman. Eventually he changed his name to Sean and became a full-fledged man. A damn good-looking man, ripped, and tattooed. I moved away to

Nashville, but I saw his photos on Facebook—both the photos he took as an acclaimed photographer and the photos of himself which he posted. He was hot. My girl crush had become something else entirely.

Maybe Just Tired

Oh whatever, I said
I can't even!
Throwing a shoe
Contemplating my age...
How can 51 seem so young and yet
So old
Filled with pain, back and knees
A mortgage and college loans
For the youngest who still likes
Her breakfast made for her
Every day
She looks just like I used to
The boys just like their dad
They drink and smoke while
We go to anonymous meetings
In empty churches
In my car I scream along with Kurt Cobain
While plotting my escape
Just like 30 years haven't passed
Just like when I threw my
Watch at him in a drunken rage
Back in 1987

Before my parents went to heaven
Before my back broke
Before I became serene
Or maybe just tired

THE END

Author Nadia Bruce-Rawlings uses grains of her once gritty life to infuse her stories with cathartic realism. She grew up travelling the world and living in various countries before settling in Los Angeles. There she briefly worked at a vitamin factory and then began a long career in the film industry. In recovery since 1998 from drugs, alcohol and an abusive but privileged upbringing, she and her husband have now settled into the Nashville area, where she writes by the lake when she can escape their five kids and dog.

Her stories "Fire" and "Scars" were both finalists in *Glimmer Train's* writing contests. Her anthology SCARS was published by Punk Hostage Press. Her story "Peace Accord" was featured in the Spring 2018 edition of *Bluestem Magazine*. In addition, she and fellow author Lois Berg co-wrote a song featured in a theatrical event they created and starred in, called "Battered But Not Broken," which was a Critic's Pick in the *Nashville Scene*. The show debuted at The Darkhorse Theatre as a fundraiser for battered women.

MORE PUNK HOSTAGE PRESS BOOKS

Fractured (2012) by Danny Baker

By A. Razor
Better Than A Gun In A Knife Fight (2012)
Drawn Blood: Collected Works From D.B.P.LTD.,
1985-1995 (2012)
Beaten Up Beaten Down (2012)
Small Catastrophes In A Big World (2012)
Half- Century Status (2013).
Days Of Xmas Poems (2014)

By Iris Berry
The Daughters Of Bastards (2012)
All That Shines Under The Hollywood Sign (2019)

Impress (2012) by C.V. Auchterlonie

Tomorrow, Yvonne - Poetry & Prose For Suicidal Egoists (2012)
by Yvonne De la Vega

Miracles Of The Blog: A Series (2012)
by Carolyn Srygley- Moore

8th & Agony (2012) by Rich Ferguson

By Jack Grisham
Untamed (2013)
Code Blue: A Love Story ~ Limited Edition (2014)
Code Blue: The Hide Under the Mattress Edition (2020)

By Dennis Cruz
Moth Wing Tea (2013)
The Beast Is We (2018)

*Blood Music (*2013) by Frank Reardon

MORE PUNK HOSTAGE PRESS BOOKS

Showgirl Confidential (2013) by Pleasant Gehman

Stealing The Midnight From A Handful Of Days (2014) by
Michele McDannold

Yeah, Well... (2014) by Joel Landmine

History Of Broken Love Things (2014) by SB Stokes

Dreams Gone Mad With Hope (2014) by S.A. Griffin

How To Take A Bullet And Other Survival Poems (2014) by

Hollie Hardy   *Dead Lions* (2014) by A.D. Winans

Scars (2014) by Nadia Bruce- Rawlings

*WHEN I WAS A DYNAMITER, Or, how a Nice Catholic Boy
Became a Merry Prankster, a Pornographer, and a Bridegroom
Seven Times* (2014) by Lee Quarnstrom.

By Alexandra Naughton
I Will Always Be Your Whore/Love Songs For Billy Corgan (2014)
*You Could Never Objectify Me More Than I've Already
Objectified Myself* (2015)

No Parachutes To Carry Me Home (2015) by Maisha Z Johnson

#1 Son And Other Stories (2017) by Michael Marcus

LOOKING FOR JOHNNY, The Legend of Johnny Thunders (2018)
by Danny Garcia

Burden Of Concrete (2020) by William S. Hayes

Dillinger's Thompson (2020) by Todd Moore